The Whole Self

Awakening The Inner Wisdom To Live as Yourself

Erin E. Brown

ISBN: 979-8-9930184-0-9
Wholeness Wisdom LLC
Asheville, NC
Erin E. Brown
www.wholenesswisdom.com

Around me the trees stir in their leaves

and call out, "Stay awhile."
The light flows from their branches.
And they call again, "It's simple," they say,
"And you too have come
into the world to do this, to go easy, to be filled
with light, and to shine."

-When I Am Among the Trees
Mary Oliver

For Tobias
What honor to have come to know
my friend, no other,
my Self

Table Of Contents

Preface to the Second Edition

In a world increasingly shaped by fragmentation—of thought, identity, and humanity—it has become both urgent and healing to remember the wholeness that has never truly been lost. This book was written as a gentle invitation back to that wholeness. Not as a concept, but as a living breathing truth.

What follows is not a manual for self-improvement or another framework for becoming someone new. The program of self-help has only perpetuated the fragmented experience of the modern person. Instead, it is a guide to recognizing what has always been present beneath the layers of conditioning: the undivided awareness that quietly animates every experience.

Through psychological insight, somatic attention, and the language of direct experience, I hope to illuminate a path toward your inherent unity. These chapters explore what it means to see the parts within us—not to fix or fight them—but to listen, understand, and include them in the larger field of awareness.

This second print edition is a living testament to the expression of choice that remains with an awakened approach to life. We do not fall at the feet of oppression in a helplessly surrendered posture, in the face of violence, but instead can invoke choice through noncompliance. Stepping into the shoes of those performing violence with compassion while walking the path of ahimsa, which Ghandi so earnestly walked, is natural when living as the Whole Self.

This second print is a response to the monopoly on publishing that Amazon and its affiliates have, and the revocation of the first edition, an example of learning as I go. Nothing in nature is perfect except the wholeness that stands at center, unmoving and yet evolving through each of us. Parts wake up to different levels of awareness every moment, while the Whole is itself unaffected. What is affected is the innocence (or ignorance,) of a perspective when it is brought to light that current actions are causing harm through negligence or seemingly passive support.

If the first edition of The Whole Self was supporting corporations that are funding active militarization, violence, oppression and/or dehumanization efforts, let that cease today. There doesn't need to be shame around the circumstances of how clarity comes to pass, though there can be a continuous openness to change.

It is possible to allow seeing our reflection in a more clarified way, and to let that be what guides change. This attitude of ahimsa is reflected in the silent prayer that I invoke with every breath:

God, Gaia, Life…help me see what is really going on.

The ideas in this book are not meant to remain theoretical. They are lived. I ask only your openness and curiosity. If anything given in this book resonates, let that be your guide— not the specific suggestions, concepts, or practices.

You are Reality. You are not separate. And there is nothing to achieve to be whole.

This is a journey of remembrance and discovery.

Thank You.
Erin

Introduction

Wholeness is the basis on which many wisdom traditions rest. Mystics, poets— even physicists—use this word to describe the foundation of who and what we are. Where words fail, religion often agrees, saying we are God's creation, and that God itself includes everything. How else to call this view than holistic? Even atheists and agnostics agree that the totality of the universe is holistic or inclusive. What could be excluded? This is an obvious yet often overlooked point.

When broadly considering the evolution of thought—apart from the limited realms of blind faith and dogmatic belief—we find that many areas of science and ancient traditions lead us to the same place: the universe seems to be one.

This book is inspired by my own personal journey through trauma, separation, and a sense of dissociation from body, mind, and self that lasted for much of my life. After coming to terms with my inability to solve this deep sense of lack on my own, I found help through community support, therapeutic supervision, and centuries-old wisdom traditions.

Though I first believed therapy and medical attention could save my life, they addressed only the physical results of an overwhelming meaninglessness.

Then came a moment—not prompted by any obvious external or internal circumstances—when a powerful insight struck me like an arrow hitting the center of a target: Come home, it seemed to say. Turn toward yourself.

Deeply influenced by the Buddhist monk and teacher Thich Nhat Hanh, I was familiar with the ideas of mindfulness and awareness. Yet during this dark time, when childhood trauma reverberated through my life, mindfulness felt distant and abstract. Meditation had been my friend, but when depression struck, it became a frightening adversary. I couldn't bear to sit with myself.

Not long after my glimpse of that arrow-strike moment, I received a serendipitous invitation from a friend. This is when I learned about self-inquiry and a unique meditative form of this used in therapeutic work. For a moment, my curiosity outweighed my skepticism.

"Can you tell me more about this?" I asked. "I've been doing meditation, but I'm not in a good place."

Instead of explaining, my friend offered to guide me through a self-inquiry session.

My doubtful mind wasn't strong enough to interrupt the process. The protestations of thought fell away the moment I truly looked for what I was asked to find. My friend's question was simple:

"Where is what you have been calling 'I'?"

Before I had an experiential view of awareness as the field of experience, I thought awareness was simply my mind focusing on something other than thoughts. But in that self-inquiry meditation, I experienced awareness as the very field in which all of my experience continually unfolded—flowing and alive.

For those whose identity is rooted in mind or body, awareness may seem like a mental state or a physical relaxation. But for me, it was immediately clear: this was a reality I was inextricably part of, inseparable from—a reality beyond mind and body.

This is the field of experience: the reality of being that we know as awareness.

It is my hope that readers will be inspired to come to their own conclusions through simple, everyday awareness, just as I was when first introduced to self-investigation. This is the science of first-person direct experiencing—and you already have everything you need to begin now.

Chapter 1

Jung, Archetypes, and The Whole Self

Defining Ourselves as Something Limited

There are many misconstrued identities that we take to be ourselves as we go through development in early life. Anyone can see that a newborn or a one-year-old child is unconditioned from identity—the personality. It turns out this person that we shape ourselves to be in development plays a role in the way we suffer in adulthood. When we define ourselves in such rigid and definite ways, we constrain ourselves to a very small space. The idea that we are inside a brain—perhaps the most widespread assumption in society today—illustrates just how small we believe ourselves to be.

Jung's Archetypes of the Psyche

Carl Gustav Jung, the father of analytic psychology, drew from Platonic ideas to identify common mental forms shared among people. He called these archetypes—universal structures of the psyche. Though these forms share a common architecture, they are expressed uniquely through each individual.

The Persona: The Social Mask

A holistic view of self includes every part. Archetypes are parts of the psyche, and the psyche is a part of the self. The persona is one such archetype identified by Carl Jung. It is the externalized self—the image or mask we present to the world.

The persona helps us function in society, establish roles, perform tasks efficiently, and distinguish ourselves from others.

Though others often take the persona at face value, it is common for people to adopt the persona as their core identity, "more or less." While there may be inner thoughts, feelings, and behaviors that remain hidden, the outward-facing mask is frequently mistaken for the whole self.

The Shadow: Hidden Parts

Another key archetype is the shadow. Jung described the shadow as the unclear, indirect aspects of ourselves that we intentionally hide from the world. The shadow often appears in dreams, typically in the form of another person.

It contains traits, thoughts, and beliefs the persona deems unattractive, dangerous, or negative. Though just as integral to the self as the persona, the shadow is harder to confront. Like the persona, it serves a purpose: to bring into conscious awareness the parts of ourselves that have been repressed, rejected, or denied.

A common misconception is that the shadow only contains what is "bad" or shameful, often linked to trauma or past mistakes. In truth, everyone has a shadow. It is not inherently negative and recognizing it is essential to knowing one's true nature.

Similarly, a major misconception about the persona is that it is the closest representation of who we are. This is dangerous because it appeals to our preference for convenience and our biological inclination to conserve energy.

Duality Blinds Us to the Holistic Self

Biology and its energy-saving tendencies can obscure our experience of wholeness. The body, requiring great energy to maintain, has evolved to generalize perception, thought, and behavior for efficiency. While this serves survival, it can be limiting.

When we move beyond this convenience, we can examine our specific archetypes and discover what obstructs the experience of a unified self. Misidentifying with a fragmented or deficient self leads to a personality built around an emptiness that cannot be resolved.

Exploring Parts: A New Approach

Archetypes reveal common psychological structures that can help us understand ourselves more fully. They merely simplify a vast array of parts into general categories. Some present-day therapies (IFS, Gestalt, SE) explore "parts"—inner subpersonalities with distinct viewpoints and experiences. Just like Jung sorting archetypes, they sort common parts into categories such as "protector," "pleaser," and "vulnerable child." Even without doing parts work, most of us can identify parts that fit these descriptions. A parts-centered approach is especially helpful in processing early life trauma.

Identifying parts is a radical step toward self-realization because it challenges the assumption that we are a singular mind or personality. It also acknowledges the fragmented way many people experience themselves. The goal in this work is to identify more often as a resourceful central-self or access what is called self-energy. This teaches a person that it is possible to keep parts in abeyance while maintaining an open dialogue and willingness to be there for them. Self-energy is a more highly resourced, mature form of oneself. However, this is often still experienced as fragmentary.

The Prevalence of Inner Duality

Inner duality is so common it often goes unnoticed. For example, one part may want to attend a concert and be social, while another part prefers solitude. This internal conflict illustrates how different parts have distinct views and preferences.

The mind often generalizes opposing viewpoints into the illusion of a single, unified personality. But this single inner self doesn't have an existence aside from the idea of it. When we openly observe a presenting part, it's possible to not identify with any aspect of it or any other part. Pure perceiving isn't identified with anything. Instead, we are experiencing from the vantage point of awareness.

Just as each part has a unique perspective, awareness does too—a singular, unifying one. We do not have a single personality inside of us that contains parts; rather, a single, unified awareness contains the whole of experience. In contrast to parts therapy models, this Self is not separate from everything in and around us. It is not an inner self but is much vaster and free of any limitation.

Jung's Process of Individuation

Carl Jung's contributions to psychology and human behavior are unparalleled. He spent his life researching culture, the unconscious, and the structure of the psyche. Through both study and countless hours in analysis, he arrived at a profound insight: the process of individuation.

Individuation is the integration of all aspects of the self—conscious and unconscious—into a transformed, unified whole. It is the resolution of inner duality and the realization of wholeness. Individuation is fragmentation coming to know itself as unified in the wholeness of

Self. While not explicitly saying that self is not contained in the body, Jung maintained that the psyche is not a process of the brain or the body but is intimately connected with what we call the outer world. His distinction between self and world was not defined by the beliefs held by the general population.

Recognizing inner parts and learning about the authentic Self through the direct experience of awareness is the most straightforward way to participate in the natural movement toward individuation— the unfolding wholeness of life itself.

Chapter 2

Reference Points and the Nature of Awareness

Distinguishing Parts from Awareness

Making a distinction between parts and awareness may be one of the simplest yet most profound things we can do. It begins with recognizing who—or what—is defining a situation. That one is always a fragment: something that stands a-part from the whole experience. A part is a lens, a specific viewpoint that interprets reality from a limited angle.

Parts can be identified by the emotions they express, the thoughts that arise, or the actions they prompt. As mentioned earlier, parts can hold contradictory views and preferences. For example, the experience of feeling offended brings a particular posture, inner dialogue, and emotional charge, whereas embarrassment carries its own unique physical and mental signature.

Parts are patterns—habitual responses to familiar situations. While deeply intertwined with experience, they remain separate from it. The internal narrative implies this part is me. When a part is active, this implication can be extremely subtle. In fact, the mental voice rarely declares "this is me I'm talking about!" Yet if it is possible to recognize something within as having a reference point, it is a part. Though it may claim or suggest to be us, or the whole self, it is blinded to its limits.

Having a reference point defines a part. Different parts have different points of view, which means they give meaning to situations in differing ways. That there is more than one internal point of view is obvious for most people. Upon reflection this shows how we don't experience a single reference point but rather hold a collection of varying lenses that express differing views depending on the situation.

Each person contains an array of contrasting perspectives.

Awareness Has No Reference Point

Unlike parts, awareness has zero reference point. It is ever-present with and within experience, without qualification or distinction. Awareness cannot be defined by traits or preferences, and its nature only becomes apparent in contrast to the parts that do possess such qualities. Talking about awareness is tricky because words attempt to put limits on what has no limitations.

In this light, the distinction between parts and awareness is surprisingly clear: anything that comes and goes, that begins and ends, is not awareness.

The phrase "The Tao that can be told is not the eternal Tao" is a famous opening line from the Tao Te Ching, a foundational text in Taoism. Awareness is the Tao. Anything with a limit or a distinction is not awareness. As we notice changing experiences, we are also simultaneously in contact with what never changes. Awareness is that constant background—the space in which all experience is known.

When we say awareness has its own point of view, (or that it is *space-*) we mean this in the same way quantum physics talks about entanglement: nothing exists alone. Awareness is the simultaneous reality of all possible points of view, manifest and in potential. Simultaneity doesn't even capture the essence of what awareness is because occurrences that are "simultaneous" only have meaning in time. Awareness is not in time.

The Futility of Seeking Awareness

Attempting to find awareness as if it were an object or a thing is not only futile, but it also reinforces separation. Awareness is ever-present, so seeking it is an exercise in redundancy. Still, the very act of openness to awareness can be transformative. When we search for a reference point for awareness we find none, and in doing so we are recognizing awareness.

This exercise, while paradoxical, helps highlight the contrast between the fragmented self and the simplicity of being. Parts are what we can look at. Awareness is what we look from.

Parts Are Dynamic, Awareness Is Constant

Parts are dynamic—they arise and pass in a flowing stream of emotions, thoughts, and impulses. No matter how hard we try to hold on to a state, it changes. This impermanence reveals something essential: that which changes cannot be the whole self. The true self—if it is to be whole— must be not subject to disappearance.

Awareness is that unchanging background. It was present before identity, and it remains even when we forget it. When we recognize it now, in the present moment, there is an immediate shift. This happens when we stop identifying with a part and return to being the wholeness of awareness.

Many of us have spent years—and significant resources—trying to understand our parts. We give them names, histories, and motivations, hoping to change or eliminate them. But parts are constructed in response to need. They are strategies—coping mechanisms that help navigate a world of shifting experiences while preserving energy and a sense of control. This is why it has been said before in this book that parts are habits. They aren't people, and in fact what we are dismantling is that very concept.

Though many coping strategies are harmless, some can be deeply disruptive. Addiction, compulsive behavior, emotional avoidance, and chronic distraction (like doom-scrolling) are all examples of negatively adapted parts trying to offer solutions. Even parts we don't like originally showed up attempting to achieve something positive.

Many approaches to working with parts recognize that all parts originate offering solutions and only afterward become a problem. Many parts therapies work to build a compassionate foundation in the person doing the work. Replacing the problem behavior with kindness toward the part is a typical goal. What is even more useful is complete integration of a part into the whole, which is less typical. Integrating parts allows a person to experience themselves wholly without a sense of inner division. Why would we stop at kindness toward the part when we have the option to allow it to no longer be separate altogether?

What Therapy Often Misses

Parts work teaches people how to talk with parts, which is a profound practice. Many people have never realized this kind of dialogue is even possible. The shift happens when we stop trying to change these parts and instead begin to listen.

Listening

Listening—particularly in an open and undirected way—is a powerful tool. Listening is different from hearing; it is pure sensing. This is a gift many of us neglect to offer ourselves. Sensing goes beyond the mental level and brings us into direct contact with experience. Shifting from analysis to pure perceiving allows more space for whatever is ready to be seen.

A listening approach is different to other methods centered on healing. In traditional talk therapy, thoughts are used to generate better, more helpful thoughts. The focus is to change thinking patterns to improve perspectives and increase positivity. However, in sensing-based work, we go to a level of being that exists *prior* to thought. There is no pressure to change experience. Using force increases division, therefore a different tack is needed for true integration.

Even Parts Work Maintains the Small Self

Parts work such as those mentioned above often miss an essential truth- if we are maintaining any division inside, we are not able to live as our full capacity. Though it isn't explicit within the process, parts are often explored with an aim to understand them better and then left to just hang out and stay there. They are often encouraged to rest in an inner place of peace we build for them, able to "come out" and express when they want or need to. The problem is the fact that parts are not anything more than contractions of the nervous system that take energy to maintain. If they are defined and then stored in an idyllic inner-place they are still maintaining pressure in the system.

When these tensions discover they can relax into a more spacious capacity than the "place" we imagine for them, we truly get back the energy that has held their position so tightly. The challenge with IFS is that even after recognizing there are many parts, the belief that we are a shell with a "me" inside is never challenged. In truth we are much more.

Chapter 3

The Unconscious: A Resource

The Active Unconscious

We live in both conscious and unconscious realms of experience. Yet the unconscious is not absent. It is alive and active, shaping behavior in unseen ways.

Consider the act of driving: at first, every movement is deliberate. Over time, these movements become second nature. Though we no longer think about pressing the pedals or steering, the knowledge hasn't disappeared—it's simply gone unconscious. The ability to drive is present, even when not actively known.

In the same way, parts we don't consciously see still operate beneath the surface. Their patterns are active, and their influence is felt.

Muscle memory is a great example. What is it, really? It isn't something stored in the muscle; it's front and center in experience, taking the form of sensations, impulses, and vague impressions. Jung observed that the psyche includes both conscious and unconscious contents. Unconscious contents are not outside of experience; we simply encounter them differently.

Seeing the Invisible

Some unconscious processes remain hidden for the practical purpose of energy efficiency. Others are actively repressed by parts that are trying to cope. Repression itself is an attempt toward peace—again, the behavior of a part.

One of Jung's greatest contributions was his work on the unconscious. He identified the many ways it expresses itself. The unconscious doesn't speak in words; it speaks in subtle cues—what we might call a gut feeling, or a vague emotional impression.

These impressions may seem small, but they impact us strongly. The psyche is inclined toward harmony, so what is not harmonious within makes itself known through discomfort, pain, and the emotional responses of the unconscious. Whether in the form of dream images or bodily sensations, unconscious material reveals itself continuously—not always in the way the mind expects.

Using the Unconscious as a Doorway to Wholeness

Both known and unknown barriers to wholeness must be investigated if we are to make an earnest attempt at being who we are. When we meet these blocks with authentic presence, they can dissolve into the capacity of the Self.

Because unconscious material often presents to us as sensations, working directly with these sensations is a highly effective practice. Thankfully, this doesn't require us to trace beliefs back to their origins. In many cases, there may be no conscious origin to find.

Instead of exhausting ourselves trying to understand everything intellectually, we can recognize the freedom that comes from letting go of that need. This surrender marks a profound maturity.

Before beginning any inner exploration, it can be helpful to consciously set the intellect aside.

Find an invitation that feels right to you. An example may be something like:

This is a space for subtle experience, thought and memory are invited to rest in the background now as I invite listening and presence for what is here.

This kind invitation clears space for a deeper kind of listening—not listening for anything but listening in an undirected way.

This listening places us at the awake and attentive center of a field of consciousness that hears.

Chapter 4

The Illusion of Separateness

A Shared Origin

All people share the same origin: birth from a womb into experience. When observing a young child—it's clear they experience the world differently than older children and adults. This difference lies in their unconditioned state. Newborn babies interact with their mothers as if she were their own body. For the baby, when a toy leaves the field of view it no longer exists. When a baby explores a color, a texture, another person's face or their own body, we witness wonder and awe—pure awareness.

This total presence is contagious. People love witnessing babies because it reminds us of our infinite capacity. It also gives us insight into what is not present for the infant—namely, separation.

This wonderful freedom is our natural state.

Around the age of two, most children begin to express a shift in perspective. They begin to differentiate themselves from their surroundings. The structure of "I" forms around ideas of right and wrong, good and bad, wanted and not wanted.

Though conceiving our environment has many advantages, it is important to recognize that all people share the same origin of pure awareness, not separate from anything. In returning to this origin, we're not finding a new self; we are remembering an essential self that has been forgotten. By removing layers of conditioned identity, we find wholeness at the center. Contraction wants to relax into the spaciousness that we are born knowing. This process is merely an invitation for tension to return to its natural state. Integrating the blocks to our whole Self makes it possible to experience unconditioned awareness all the time. This is possible without sacrificing resourcefulness or functionality.

Awareness Is Not Part of Duality

Exploring wholeness begins with recognizing what is fragmented and noticing what is constant. Fragmentation is dualistic. "Dual" means two, implying separation. Anything dual can be defined and measured. Science is a tool designed for measurement and abstraction.

Science, as an extension of our sensory perception, measures the world in values and abstractions for the purpose of predicting outcomes. Science maps objective reality, but it cannot be used to explore subjective experience. Subjective experience is private and directly experienced with no room for abstraction. Unfortunately, many assume that investigating the non-dual is unscientific. On the contrary, it is a form of science— the science of the first person. This approach is the most direct and accessible because it begins with what is closest: direct experience. Awareness can only be known through first-person experiencing.

The Science of the First Person

Just as a map is used to explore a specific region, third-person science explores an objective world. But the map is not the territory. The scientific process is objective and predictive, but subjective exploration is directly perceived and immediate.

The science of first-person experience emphasizes perception over measurement. In self-inquiry, noticing our direct perceptions becomes a kind of map guiding us back to the richness of the territory—our experience. At the core of experience lies the self that is infinite, and we do not need to go somewhere to find it. The territory is closer than close.

Chapter 5

Awareness in Daily Life

Living as Awareness

Some frameworks describe awakening in stages. One such model maps the progression as follows:

Life happens…

1. to me
2. for me
3. by me
4. as me

This last stage can be realized with a simple glimpse of our true nature. Being non-linear, these stages may not happen as the mind expects they will.

Though parts of us may experience awakening as a progression, the truth of life happening "as me" is always present—

even when parts are unaware of it.
Awareness is not limited even by time.
Awareness is already here, already whole.
We don't need to build or progress toward
it.
We only recognize it, if it wants to be
known.

Losing Interest

Living as awareness (life as me) or the true
Self doesn't rely on personal advancement.
This unfolds according to a natural
movement. As noticing continues to occur
more often, life wakes up to itself and
what we used to think of as a personal self
is present to enjoy the ride. Some spiritual
traditions offer helpful pointers that
sometimes hasten our recognition of this
truth. Over time, this recognition becomes
preferred—not through effort, but
through increased curiosity.

This shift often leads to a gentle loss of
interest in limited perspectives. Instead of
striving or forcing change, we simply stop
caring about the false view. This is
effortless, natural, and freeing. Direct

experience reveals our completeness and makes this path attractive, easy, and worthwhile.

The Sanskrit term for losing interest is *vairagya*, which translates to losing interest in that which is not eternal. Ironically, after losing interest in this way many people report richer depth of feeling, more intimate relationships, and increased joy.

The Final Stage of Maturity

Children are often asked what they want to be when they grow up. They learn to equate self-worth with identities and accomplishments. But what if they were taught to acknowledge and celebrate the simple fact of being?

True maturity goes beyond concepts of self. To reach it, we must recognize and let go of false identities. Conceiving oneself is an abstraction; perceiving the Self is reality. We can walk-back and reverse the algorithm that blinds us to the direct experience of being.

Chapter 6

Life Beyond Concepts

Conceiving Ourselves

Imagine the developing child layering concepts of self like rubber bands forming a ball. The ball seems like a single thing, but it's only layers. Similarly, what we call "me" is just a collection of self-concepts. What remains when the layers fall away?

Tapping into Curiosity

To investigate the true self, curiosity is essential. Zen Buddhism honors "beginner's mind" as a very high state—looking from a place of not-knowing. If we start with preconceptions about what we are, our looking is clouded right away. We must see as a child does. When seeing for the very first time, without firmly held ideas about ourselves, we can honestly look to find if there is anything there without these ideas.

Beyond Concepts

Looking at the self beyond concepts is a rediscovery. We have an innate right to an unburdened existence. Life this way is full of clarity. It is possible to see through false self-images without guilt or judgment, and to just be, knowingly. It means flowing with and as life rather than resisting it. This shift has many implications, some big and some small, but it always is known foremost in our private experience. No one can realize the self through someone else's experience.

The First Turning

Self-inquiry is a process that emphasizes perceiving. It is a qualitative process of sensing and observing. Turning ourselves toward awareness doesn't require exercises or meditative postures! In fact, it is best when made a simple part of daily life. Sticky note reminders, brief moments of checking in, or simply resting as awareness before falling asleep are all ways to familiarize checking into the presence of awareness throughout the day. The simplest way is to ask, "Am I aware of awareness?" and perceive the capacity of awareness directly.

Misconceptions About Awareness

Awareness doesn't take special levels of wisdom or experience to reach. A baby is born with awareness, and awareness is here for every moment of our lives. Awareness is a fact and requires no effort. It cannot be gained or lost. It doesn't need improvement—it already is.

In deep sleep there is awareness in and through the body. Even with zero-memory of deep sleep, we do not cease being. Awareness is the same as being. Some people confuse awareness for thinking, and this is a misconception. Thinking depends on our being aware, while awareness always is—with or without thought. Another confused idea about awareness is that awareness and attention are the same thing. Attention is not necessary for awareness and does not improve it. This is what many types of meditation intend to reveal. Many seekers try to cultivate awareness through effort, but this is based on confused thinking. Practices are for attention, not awareness.

Practices Are Not for Self-Improvement

Awareness is already complete in Itself and cannot be improved. Attention, however, can be redirected and trained. Practices help redirect attention inward, which is useful because attention is habitually outward going. Training attention can be done for reasons other than self-improvement; the motivation can come from a desire to see oneself fully. The idea of self-improvement is a barrier to wholeness. Self-improvement implies a lack, while turning toward oneself completely is an act of total inclusivity, coming from love. Even without the experience of love, there can be a momentum for practices fueled by the desire for truth. When arriving at this truth it is likely that the motivation to improve oneself changes or completely dissolves.

Chapter 7

Reactions and Meta-Reactions

The Deficiency of Fragmentation

A common experience of separateness is the feeling of lack. This sense of insufficiency hurts. Self-inquiry brings us face to face with the personal beliefs that maintain a sense of lack and give reality to a false self. When those beliefs are exposed and questioned something called backlash can happen. This resistance shows itself in various forms of reactions. Sometimes backlash looks like a sudden return of impulsive or emotional behavior, or old patterns of thinking.

Understanding Reactions

There are two types of reactions: primary and meta-reactions. A primary reaction resists what is happening in the moment. A meta-reaction resists the initial reaction.

For example, during self-inquiry a feeling of tightness in the chest may suddenly arise. This could be followed by a sense of fear or worry. The second feeling is a meta-reaction—it resists the first.

Why Reactions Matter

Avoiding reactions leads to suppression, which is a denial of wholeness. Including reactions is essential for recognizing the nature of who and what we are. Beliefs and reactions reinforce each other. By investigating some things and not others we only maintain inner duality. Inclusion is the direct path to lasting peace.

Chapter 8

Giving Voice to Parts

Parts Speak Through Reactions

Reactions are expressions of parts.
Offering them a voice brings unconscious
material into awareness. Just as driving
becomes unconscious over time, so too
can beliefs. Self-inquiry gives us tools to
listen and uncover what was hidden.

The Science of Listening

Self-inquiry is both an art and a science. It
begins with a question and dissolves into
listening. The goal is not to find the
"right" answer, but to open space for
awareness. Repetition is key.

Questions for Inquiry

Here are some questions you might explore. Remember, exploring is not seeking any result.

- Am I aware?

- What is the size of awareness?

- Has awareness ever been affected by an emotion? A thought?

- Is awareness full or empty?

Listening To Parts

To listen to a part, begin by locating it in the body. Often a part is a sensation that is felt associated with a sense of "me," "I" or "my." It may also arise with a specific thought.

Ask:

What are you experiencing?

What is your view of the world, me, and life?

What is the belief underneath this feeling?

What are you missing?

What are you believing is true?

Don't seek answers or attempt to understand or form a narrative; just be the space of listening.

Any reaction that arises is included. The point of asking questions to parts is to experience them without any motivation other than to recognize their perspective. Recognizing this from the perspective of awareness, is a profound practice. This is the dance of inquiry—being the space where unconscious parts meet the harmonizing presence of awareness.

Over time, the limited perspectives of parts dissolve into that which is larger and freer. This happens not by force but by nature. With perseverance and motivation for greater truth this practice can unveil a lightness that draws everything we've longer for to the experiential center. This is the harmonizing nature of wholeness itself.

Deeper Contemplation

After uncovering an answer in the form of a belief it is extremely useful to contemplate this using a deeper and quite precise method of contemplation. In this one asks repeatedly if this belief is true.

This process was developed by Helen Hamilton and more can be found about it on helenhamilton.org.

To begin this practice, sit in a comfortable place and ask

Is it really true that....

finishing the question with the belief to be contemplated.

It is important to remain in the undirected listening space without trying to qualify answers as good or bad. Many answers will arise in response to this, each time simply return to the question.

Eventually the response will shift in a way that releases the charge.

Chapter 9

The Body Narrative—Somatic Inquiry

When Language Isn't the Way In

Any reaction, part, or difficult emotion can be approached in two primary ways: through inquiry that uses language, and through inquiry that does not. Both are valid paths toward presence.

Somatic styles of inquiry are a form of parts work, with the only difference being that they use sensation—not words—as the bridge to awareness. In this way we could say that any sensation is approached as a part. As we explored in chapter 2, parts are habits of the nervous system. Responding to patterns in a new way, (by perceiving them as awareness instead of as the pattern) relieves tension that has been held in the nervous system—releasing the charge.

The Effort-Less Approach

Because awareness has a limitless capacity, it is common for these patterns to dissolve completely once they have been processed with somatic inquiry. However, using inquiry as a way to make something go away is a misguided approach. Striving toward an outcome will not bring us to the whole Self—striving is a form of denial. Instead, it is worth celebrating that an effortless approach is the most effective.

Using sensation as a doorway to wholeness requires simply the willingness to notice what is experienced. We begin this by exploring the body. Sensations are always qualitative, meaning they have an immediate quality of experience that is present when noticed.

The following page lists examples of sensation qualities.

It feels…

fuzzy
vibrating
static
dense
heavy
warm
prickly
diffuse
humid
noisy
silent
cool
light
etc.

There may be visual aspects that are also
sensation qualities.

It looks…

rough
cavernous
metallic
scratchy
sparkly
bright
dark

fuzzy
shiny
woven
etc.

Setting Aside Interpretation

Somatic styles of inquiry are easiest when
checking into the quality rather than the
interpretation that may arise with it. If a
narrative emerges during inquiry about a
sensation, such as its scared, simply check
for the sensation that is experienced in the
location that was called scared.

This type of inquiry is especially useful
when stress is high, thoughts are
overwhelming, or language feels like too
much effort. The sensory path simply
takes noticing. Whenever there is a story
or narrative there is no need to judge it or
deny it. Simply return to noticing. There is
always the option of exploring what is
happening as a sensation.

Practicing Somatic Inquiry

Somatic inquiry begins with the simplest turning inward, toward immediate perceptions. Whatever is in present experience is the right place to begin. There are no special requirements—no need to be in a calm mood or specific posture. You can practice this while sitting in your car, standing in line, or lying in bed.

The Basic Steps of Somatic Inquiry

1. Start by inviting stillness and follow by pausing any activity.

2. Close your eyes. This isn't required but can support inward attention.

3. Next, notice any sensation in or around the body that stands out. It might be a tension in the chest, a

flutter in the belly, or a vague
contraction. *

4. Invite attention to include the wider
    field that the sensation is in. Allow
    the intention to be to recognize
    awareness through and all around
    this sensation. The division between
    sensation and awareness may
    naturally dissolve or there may be
    an experience of anything
    "separate" being one single
    sensation.

*Note: If the top layer of experience is a
thought, find out where exactly the
thought is experienced. Then notice the
sounds or images—the *sensations*—that
arise with it.

This simple process relies direct
experience. Direct experiencing is what
somatic inquiry is. It is about total
inclusion. Going forward in the spirit of
curiosity greatly supports being open for
whatever happens.

You don't need to name what happens or analyze anything—just notice from an undirected listening position. Notice if the sensation changes when it is allowed to coexist and even merge with the awareness that is available.

Exploring the Body Like a Story

The identity we believe in is like a living narrative. Just as stories have characters, settings, and plots, our lived experience carries familiar elements: the recurring roles we play (the persona), the conflicting ones (shadows), the external setting of our lives, and the active narration through time (the 'inner voice'/ memories).

Just Like Stories

Just like stories, our internal experience contains:

Who: what we call "I", the fragmented self

What: the perceptions related to identity

Where: the places fragmentation is experienced

When/How: the beliefs that are stored

Why: the instinctual or habitual process of fragmentation

A Layered, Step-by-Step Approach

Somatic inquiry is a useful practice for dismantling the separate sense of self. Only ideas can be reached by the mind, so exploring identity on a deeper level is necessary. The problem cannot be solved at the same level on which it was created. The story of the small self is mind-made. Therefore, we must go to the level prior to the problem—prior to the mind. By using a structured approach, layers of the limited self can be dissolved one at a time and this story can be integrated into a full experience of Self. Taking the layers listed above one-by-one, we can integrate what seems distinct and therefore separate. The goal is not to fix something, but to recognize these layers as parts of a whole, the enfolded nature of an infinite and fundamental Self that is not abstract but is lived.

Dissolving as Awareness

The final step of somatic inquiry is inviting and allowing sensations to return to the field of presence or awareness that is available. This was briefly described in step 4. in the Basic Steps listed above. This return happens by noticing and including what the sensation is experienced in, which is always awareness.
Once attention includes the field of awareness, contractions can return to their natural state. Once this possibility is offered integration happens in a variety of ways.

Integration is different for everyone. It may feel like awareness meets the sensation and merges as one with it. There may be a filling sensation, a warmth or a movement. The experience of capacity may flow to the sensation, fully absorbing it and dissolving distinction. Some people experience awareness present around, throughout, and as the sensation itself. There may be a sense of the sensation being alive as awareness or shining as itself. Do not try for any specific option above but rather be open to all of them and more. Once the possibility for integration with and as awareness is given, anything can happen. Many people report awareness is experienced as Self; whole and not separate from anything.

Chapter 10

Awareness As the Self

Awareness

Unfolding the personal narrative is about dissolving lesser truths into a higher or more fundamental truth. This is the role of awareness. Notice awareness now and see if you can find a size to it. Do you find another awareness to compare it to? No. Go ahead and try.
Can you find where your awareness ends, and another awareness begins?

Now, notice the depth or the breadth of awareness—does it start at a specific point in you and reach out to a specific point where it finally stops? What is the boundary of awareness?
There isn't an edge.

Capacity

Now, notice the capacity to notice awareness. From your capacity to notice awareness, see if you can find where you begin and awareness ends. Checking this out now, do you find another thing apart from awareness that can see it? Even if it isn't seeing with the eyes- when the eyes are shut, the looking can still happen. Look for awareness with your eyes closed and appreciate the capacity for looking that is here. This looking has a capacity— see if you can find the edge. This is your capacity, and it is one with awareness.

Notice the sounds that are happening now, some may be louder, and some may be faint. Notice the silence in which all sounds occur. Notice the size of this silence. How big is it? Can you find another to compare it to? This is the capacity in which sound can be noticed.

Now, notice the taste in your mouth. Some of this may be sweet, or sour, or very faint. The taste there now may be indescribable. There may be the remains of a flavor that seems larger than other tastes.

Now, outside of any particular taste check for the tasteless capacity that is here, the emptiness that tastes fill. Notice the capacity for tasting. This is a capacity— your capacity.

Altogether, the experiencing capacity is here. It is one single capacity. Notice the vast field of possibility that this capacity is. The whole field of experience is full of what can be noticed and is also complete in Itself; a capacity that is not full of anything at all.

This capacity is natural, and it is your Self. This capacity does not have a boundary, and it is open. This is not a separate capacity from you, noticing it. This capacity and awareness are the same. When we invite a content of experience to merge with awareness or integrate, we are including this capacity and the infinite field that it is.

The Natural State

The false self is a misunderstanding that anything happening in this capacity is who we are. Any content of the capacity is a fragment— it isn't the whole self. We mistake ourselves for a limited piece of the whole, instead of the capacity itself.

The good news is that a misunderstanding doesn't have any substance to it, it is just an idea.

Releasing Tension with Awareness

Some people play a joke where they tap the opposite shoulder of a person in front of them. When the person turns around— they see nobody there. Realizing the person who did the tapping was on their other side, the one who has been fooled sees the joke!

If we slow down this scenario, we can observe tension held in the moment of misunderstanding. As the situation unfolds, awareness meets confusion, and the tension naturally is released.

Because misunderstanding has no substance, when misunderstanding clears up nothing has changed or been affected.

It is simply an illusion that has been seen through to the truth behind it. What dissolves the illusion is awareness, which happens because awareness is a "larger" or more true capacity. Illusion cannot maintain itself when awareness meets it.

Seeing again from the example, the one fooled doesn't use effort to clear the misunderstanding. Awareness naturally dissolves illusion into itself.

No Wrong Turns

This framework for self-investigation offers simple tools to help you see the truth that you are One. If there is one thing I have learned most through guiding others in self-inquiry, it is that the details are unique for every single person! The roadmap is different because the territory varies between people. Which method and questions support your process the best can only be found by trying for yourself and seeing what happens. Please take this one message above all else: be yourself. When motivated by nothing other than your own yearning for authenticity- it is impossible to go wrong on the path to Self-discovery.

Chapter 11

A Supported Path

The Way to Unlearn is Varied

There is no prescriptive path to awakening to your whole Self, because you already are you, which is limitless awareness. Coming to see this has no impact on your already being that. The benefits that come from acknowledging who you really are worth mentioning. Attention will likely return to illusion because it is the habit to do so. It is up to you to pursue this topic in the way that fits you. It is recommended from my own experience and from working with others, that support on the path is extremely helpful and encouraging. Although wholeness is what Is and reality is That…this is not typically acceptable conversation in society today.

Joining in and receiving help from others doesn't only support Self-recognition, it's fun! People who have seen their true nature are often relaxed, authentic, encouraging, and open to talk about challenges they face. Intimacy is a beautiful experience, and it happens more often when people celebrate the facts: what we are cannot be harmed because the Self is whole.

Furthermore, deeper relationships are possible as this knowing becomes more alive in one's day-to-day, even when those we love aren't interested in seeing or sharing about Who we are.

No Fireworks

If this doesn't seem like a remarkable answer or a quick fix to the problems in your life, this is normal. It is because this topic both is and isn't remarkable. Who we are is the entire capacity of experience— wow! Finding out we don't need to become something other than our self can also feel a little disappointing for parts that are used to doing. Simply put, there isn't anything to do. What a relief!

At the same time, knowing that there is nothing to fix is remarkable! We can relax and simply be as our infinite capacity at any time!

If the goal is to become our real self, which we are already—the arrival point is just being.

Living This Way

When any obstacle to being shows up, this can dissolve into awareness through various attention-guiding practices. Still, with the knowing that we already are whole, this "problem" can also simply be seen as a part of the whole capacity that is awareness. Everything is pointing us back to the Center. Returning to the *subjective experience* of awareness naturally dissolves what was experienced as separation.

Being oneself knowingly as awareness is the easy and natural way to be the infinite Self.

When we acknowledge we Already are this open capacity the next step is to simply be, enjoy, and enjoy being our natural Self.

Resources

Support for this work can be pursued in various ways. I offer resources here for a continuation on this path to wholeness that may appeal to different levels of interest, understanding, and different personality types.

Wholeness Work and Core Transformation are deeper practices of Parts Work and Somatic Inquiry that investigate specific challenges and reveal the core of wholeness in each session. The author is a seasoned guide in both methods and much of the information in this book is informed by insights gathered through this work.

Facebook Page:
Connect Create Wholeness

Books:

Celebrating Who We Are by Richard Lang

Coming To Wholeness and
Core Transformation by Connirae Andreas
Ph.D.

The Wholeness Wisdom Podcast
with Erin E. Brown

For more info on Wholeness Work and
Core Transformation Process 1:1 Zoom
support visit
wholenesswisdom.com

The Wheel of Wholeness: Waking Up To
Your Infinite Self
An online course with group support
starting January 6th, 2026 visit
www.wholenesswisdom.com/enroll

For more courses visit:
www.wholenesswisdom.com

About The Author

Erin Brown is a guide in the integrative processes of
Wholeness Work and Core Transformation.
Since 2022 she has been working with people around
the world and inviting them to recognize their
essential nature.

Coming from addiction and recovery, Erin's own
realization has brought forth a life that is rich,
celebrated, and lends itself to sharing.

She lives in Western North Carolina, enjoying being
with her partner, their two dogs and three cats. She
can be contacted through her website
www.wholenesswisdom.com

Thank You

It is my innermost pleasure and honor to share with you and be together on this path alongside you. Please leave a review or contact me if you have found this material significant, helpful, or if you have experience to share.
Your experience is encouraging for others in an all too fragmented world.
Thank you for being true to yourself!

The greatest service you can render the world is your own self-realization.

-Ramana Maharshi

Erin E. Brown
August, 2025
Asheville, North Carolina

Glossary

Awareness
The ever-present, unified field in which all experiences unfold—distinct from thoughts, sensations, and identities.

Parts
Inner subpersonalities or lenses through which we experience life; each with its own feelings, thoughts, and viewpoints.

The Persona
One of Jung's archetypes. A social mask or image presented to the world; often mistaken for the whole self.

The Shadow
Another archetype. The repressed or hidden aspects of the self that are not consciously acknowledged but remain active in the psyche.

Individuation
Jung's term for the process of integrating all aspects of the self into a unified whole.

Self-Inquiry
A method of exploring identity by questioning and observing internal experience to reveal awareness.

Somatic Inquiry
A body-based approach to self-exploration that focuses on sensation rather than thought or language.

Meta-Reaction
A reaction to a reaction; for example, feeling anxious about being angry.

Repression
A coping strategy where parts of experience are pushed out of conscious awareness for protection.

Direct Experiencing
A mode of sensing reality through present-moment awareness without conceptual overlay.

Wholeness
The natural, undivided state of being that underlies all fragmentation and identity structures.

Fragmentation
The perception or experience of being divided or broken into parts; often a result of trauma or conditioning. This can be felt in the sense of lack.

Muscle Memory
An example of unconscious knowledge that is expressed through bodily sensation and habit.

Beginner's Mind
A Zen concept of approaching life without preconceptions, allowing openness to truth and presence.